The wonderful story of Joseph is in the Old Testament of the Bible, in the book of Genesis, where everyone can read it.

Long ago Joseph lived in the land of Canaan. He had eleven brothers. His father, Jacob, loved Joseph more than he loved his other children. He made him a special coat—a coat of many colors. This made his brothers hate Joseph.

Once Joseph dreamed he and his brothers were tying up sheaves of grain, and their sheaves bowed down to his. When he told them his dream, his brothers were furious. "We'll never bow down to you," they roared.

Later, his brothers took their father's sheep to graze away from home. Jacob sent Joseph to see how they were getting along.

When they saw Joseph coming, some of his brothers wanted to kill him. But Reuben, the oldest brother, said, "Don't kill him. Let's just throw him into a deep, dark pit." (Reuben thought he'd pull Joseph out of the pit later.) The rest agreed.

So the minute he came near they grabbed Joseph, tore off his special coat—his coat of many colors—and threw him into a deep, dark pit. They left him there.

Later, while Reuben was away, the other brothers drew Joseph out of the pit and sold him to a band of merchants who were going to Egypt on their camels.

When Reuben returned to the pit, he found Joseph gone. He told his brothers, and they tore Joseph's coat and took it home to their father. "Look what we found," they said. "Could this be Joseph's?" It is my son's coat," Jacob cried. "An evil beast must have eaten him."

Meanwhile, the merchants sold Joseph to Potiphar, an officer in the Egyptian king's army. Potiphar soon realized that God was with Joseph and made all that he did to succeed. Therefore, Potiphar put Joseph in charge of everything he owned.

Potiphar's wife took an interest in Joseph and said, "Lie with me…." "No!" he said. "How can I do this great wickedness, and sin against God? You are married to Potiphar." She was so angry that she told Potiphar lies about Joseph, and he threw Joseph into prison.

But God was with him there.

Pretty soon Joseph was put in charge of all the prisoners. Among them were two servants of Pharaoh, the Egyptian king. God helped Joseph explain some disturbing dreams these men had. Joseph said their dreams meant they would be taken out of prison in three days. He was right.

A long time afterward, Pharaoh dreamed strange dreams. In one he saw seven fat cows feeding in a field. Then seven skinny cows gobbled them up. In the other dream he saw seven plump ears of corn growing on one stalk. But seven scraggly ears ate them.

None of Pharaoh's wise men could explain these dreams. Then one of those servants who had been taken out of prison told about Joseph explaining his dream. So Pharaoh sent for Joseph right away.

Joseph said, "God is telling Pharaoh that plenty of food will grow in the next seven years. Then nothing will grow for seven years. Famine will be over all the land."

"You must store away food when it is plentiful, Pharaoh," Joseph said.

Everybody thought this was a good idea. Pharaoh said, "Because God has showed you this, Joseph, I'll put you in charge of all Egypt."

During the next seven years Joseph filled every storehouse in Egypt. Then when the famine came, the Egyptians had plenty to eat.

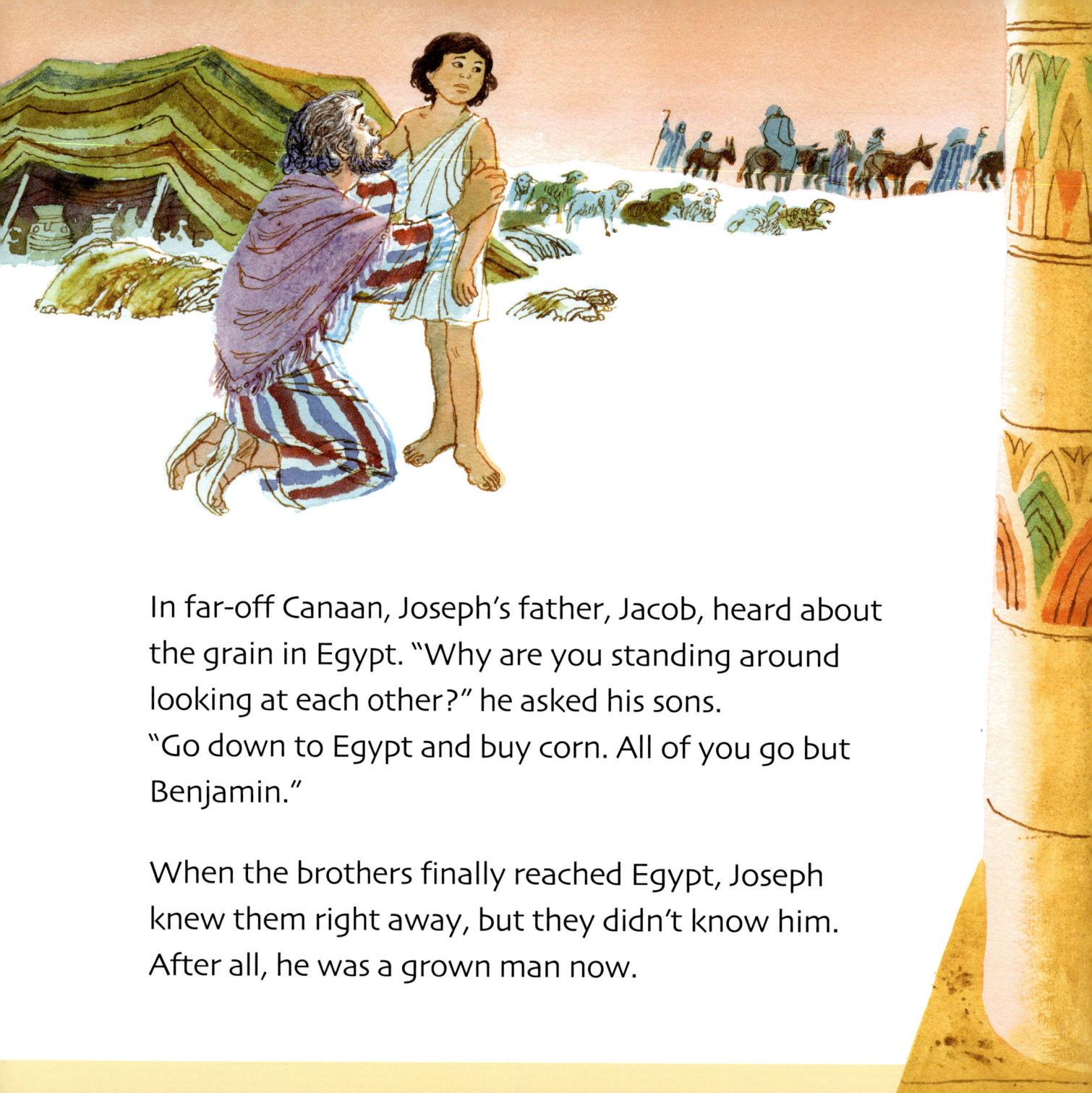

In far-off Canaan, Joseph's father, Jacob, heard about the grain in Egypt. "Why are you standing around looking at each other?" he asked his sons.
"Go down to Egypt and buy corn. All of you go but Benjamin."

When the brothers finally reached Egypt, Joseph knew them right away, but they didn't know him. After all, he was a grown man now.

Maybe Joseph wanted to see if his brothers were sorry for the way they had treated him. Anyway, he didn't tell them who he was. He pretended he thought they were spies. "We're not spies," they cried. "We just came here to buy food. Our youngest brother, Benjamin, is home in Canaan with our father, and one of our brothers disappeared."

Finally Joseph said they could buy grain and go home. "All but Simeon," Joseph said. "He must stay here, and in prison, till I'm sure you're telling the truth. Don't ever come back without Benjamin."

Imagine how Jacob felt when his sons came home without Simeon, and when they said they must take Benjamin if they returned to Egypt.
"Never," Jacob said sadly. "Joseph and Simeon are gone. I can't stand losing Benjamin, too."

When their corn was eaten, Jacob said, "You'll have to go to Egypt again." Judah spoke quickly, "The man in charge of grain won't let us come without Benjamin." So at last, because everyone was so hungry, Jacob let Benjamin go.

Joseph was delighted to see them. He invited them to dinner at his great, beautiful house, and brought Simeon to join them. They still didn't know who Joseph was.

Early the next morning Joseph's brothers started home with their grain. They hadn't gone far when Joseph's steward, or servant, overtook them.

"My master's silver cup is missing," he cried. "Whoever has it must become my master's slave."

He searched all their sacks, beginning with that of the oldest. When he came to Benjamin's sack, there was the silver cup!

Now Joseph had told his steward to hide the silver cup in Benjamin's sack; and he had sent the steward after his brothers, to test their honesty. The frightened brothers returned to Joseph's great, beautiful house.

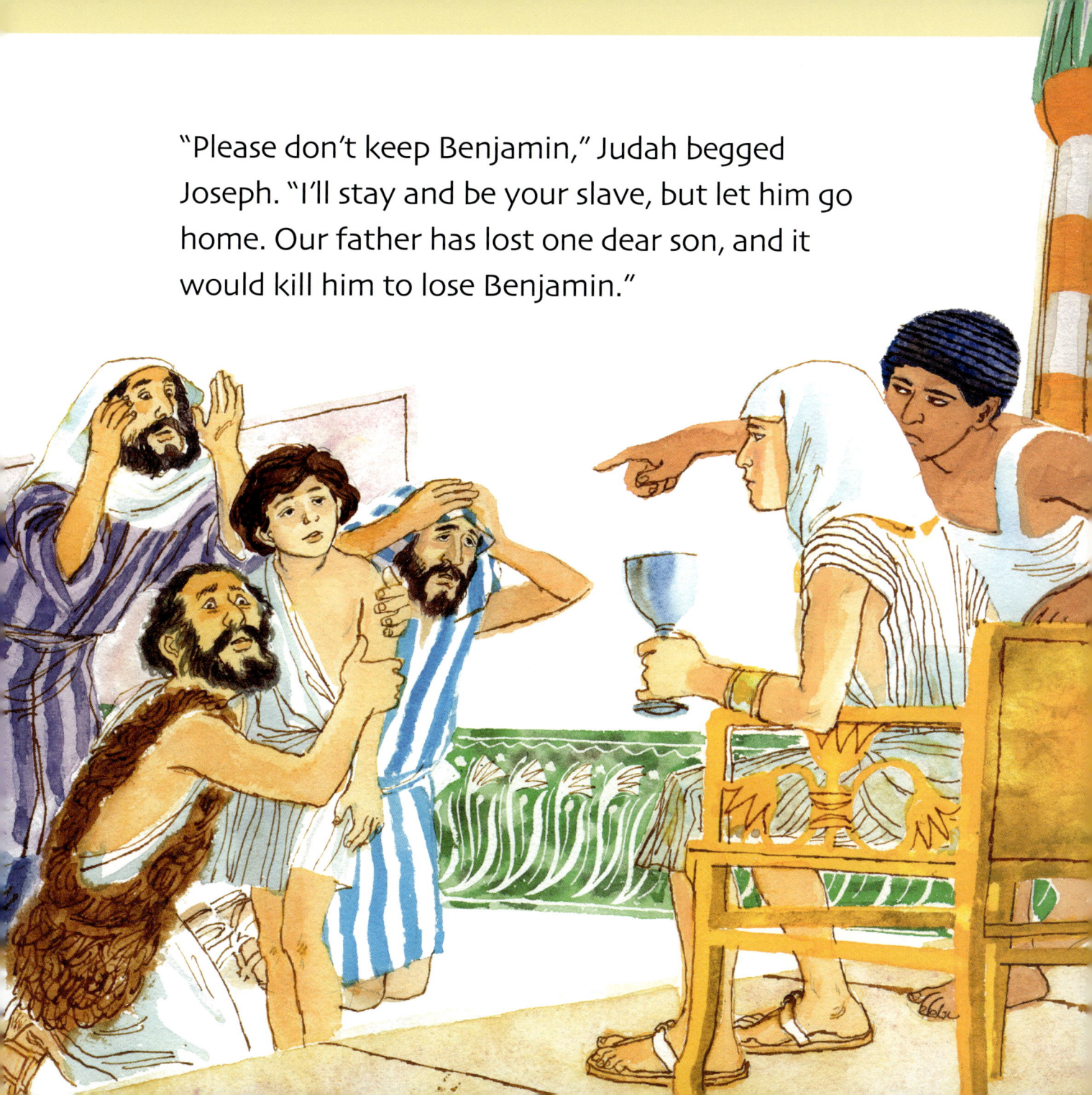

"Please don't keep Benjamin," Judah begged Joseph. "I'll stay and be your slave, but let him go home. Our father has lost one dear son, and it would kill him to lose Benjamin."

When Joseph saw how his brothers loved Benjamin and their father, he sent everyone but his brothers out of the room. "Look at me," he said. "I'm Joseph, your brother, whom you sold into Egypt."
Well, they were too surprised to speak.

"Don't feel sorry about what you did to me long ago," Joseph said.
He knew God had made him able to save all their lives.
Then Joseph kissed his brothers, and there was nothing but brotherly love between them.

When Pharaoh heard about Joseph's brothers, he was very pleased. "Send them home to get your father and their families," he told Joseph. "Tell them, 'The good of all the land of Egypt is yours.'"

Joseph trusted God. He blessed his enemies. He didn't return evil for evil. He knew God made him able to help other people—even those who tried to hurt him.

We, too, can trust God, do good, and help others.

We can be like Joseph.